P9-DMI-744

TURNING 15 ON THE
ROAD TO FREEDOM

TURNING 15 ON THE ROAD TO FREEDOM

MY STORY OF THE 1965 SELMA VOTING RIGHTS MARCH

by LYNDA BLACKMON LOWERY

as told to ELSPETH LEACOCK
and SUSAN BUCKLEY

illustrated by
PJ LOUGHRAN

speak

SPEAK
An imprint of Penguin Random House LLC
375 Hudson Street
New York, New York 10014

First published in the United States of America by Dial Books,
an imprint of Penguin Random House LLC
Published by Speak, an imprint of Penguin Random House LLC, 2016

Copyright © 2015 by Lynda Blackmon Lowery, Elspeth Leacock, and Susan Buckley
Illustrations copyright © PJ Loughran
Discussion guide copyright © 2016 by Lynda Blackmon Lowery,
Elspeth Leacock, and Susan Buckley

Penguin supports copyright. Copyright fuels creativity, encourages diverse voices,
promotes free speech, and creates a vibrant culture. Thank you for buying an
authorized edition of this book and for complying with copyright laws by not
reproducing, scanning, or distributing any part of it in any form without permission.
You are supporting writers and allowing Penguin to
continue to publish books for every reader.

THE LIBRARY OF CONGRESS HAS CATALOGED THE DIAL BOOKS EDITION AS FOLLOWS:

Lowery, Lynda Blackmon, date.
Turning 15 on the road to freedom : my story of the 1965 Selma Voting Rights March /
by Lynda Blackmon Lowery ;
as told to Elspeth Leacock and Susan Buckley ; illustrated by PJ Loughran
pages cm
ISBN 978-0-8037-4123-2
1. Selma to Montgomery Rights March (1965 : Selma, Ala.)—Juvenile literature.
2. Selma (Ala.)—Race relations-Juvenile literature. 3. African Americans—Civil
Rights—Alabama—Selma—History—20th century—Juvenile literature. 4. African
Amercans—Suffrage—Alabama—Selma—History—20th century—Juvenile literature.
5. Civil rights movements—Alabama—Selma—History—20th century—Juvenile
literature. 6. Lowery, Lynda Blackmon,
date. I. Leacock, Elspeth. II. Buckley, Susan Washburn. III. Loughran, PJ,
illustrator. IV. Title : Turning fifteen on the road to freedom.
F334.S4L69 2015   323.1196'073076145—dc3   2013047316

Speak ISBN 9780147512161

Designed by Mina Chung

Printed in the United States of America

3 5 7 9 10 8 6 4 2

For Joanne Blackmon Bland,
who brought us together,
and for the children who march for
freedom around the world

TABLE OF CONTENTS

WOKE UP THIS MORNING

Woke up this morning with my mind
Stayed on freedom
Woke up this morning with my mind
Stayed on freedom
Woke up this morning with my mind
Stayed on freedom
Hallelu. Hallelu. Hallelujah.

I'm walking and talking with my mind
Stayed on freedom
I'm walking and talking with my mind
Stayed on freedom
I'm walking and talking with my mind
Stayed on freedom
Hallelu. Hallelu. Hallelujah.

Ain't nothing wrong with my mind

Stayed on freedom

Oh, there ain't nothing wrong

with keeping my mind

Stayed on freedom

There ain't nothing wrong

with keeping your mind

Stayed on freedom

Hallelu, Hallelu, Hallelujah.

I'm singing and praying with my mind

Stayed on freedom

Yeah, I'm singing and praying with my mind

Stayed on freedom

Hallelu, Hallelu, Hallelujah.

CHAPTER 1
GROWING UP STRONG AND DETERMINED

By the time I was fifteen years old, I had been in jail nine times.

I was born in Selma, Alabama, in 1950. In those days, you were born black or you were born white in Selma—and there was a big difference.

Where I lived, *everyone* was black. I lived in the George Washington Carver Homes. My buddies and I all felt safe there because everyone watched out for one another. If one family couldn't pay the rent, the others got together and had card parties and fish fries to raise the money. Nobody talked about it afterward either, because the next month it might be you who needed help.

We went to black churches and we went to black schools, where we had caring black teachers. I looked forward to going to school.

The Ku Klux Klan stayed away from us. (They were a group of crazy white folks who hated us black people and were determined to keep us out of places—to keep us segregated.) They drove through other black neighborhoods, hiding their faces with sheets on their

heads, yelling racial slurs, blowing their horns, and cursing and shooting their guns. They rode through areas where they knew they could scare people, but they would not ride through the George Washington Carver Homes.

I felt safe and secure.

We were poor then, but I never knew it. I can't remember a day in my life when I went hungry, even after my mother died when I was seven years old. My daddy made sure of that. I loved the ground my daddy walked on. I did. When different family members wanted to take us to live with them after Mama died, Daddy said he wasn't separating his kids. He wasn't giving us to anybody. At my mother's funeral, we heard Daddy say that we were his children and he would take care of us. I was the oldest of four. Jackie was next, then Joanne, and then baby Al.

When my mother died, I heard the older people say, "If she wasn't colored, she could've been saved." But the hospital was for whites only. My mother died as a result of her skin color. I just believe that. So segregation hurt my family. It did. It hurt me.

After my mother's funeral my grandmother moved in. She was one determined woman, and she was going to raise us up to be strong

and determined too. I remember her saying as she brushed my hair, "There is nothing more precious walking on this earth than you are. You are a child of God. So hold up your head and believe in yourself."

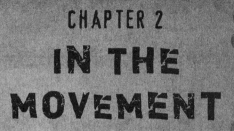

CHAPTER 2
IN THE
MOVEMENT

It was my grandmother who first took me to hear Dr. King—that's Dr. Martin Luther King Jr. That was back in 1963, when I was just thirteen years old. The church was packed. When Dr. King began to speak, everyone got real quiet. The way he sounded just made you want to do what he was talking about. He was talking about voting—the right to vote and what it would take for our parents to get it. He was

Dr. Martin Luther King Jr. Selma, January 2, 1965

talking about nonviolence and how you could persuade people to do things your way with steady, loving confrontation. I'll never forget those words—"steady, loving confrontation"— and the way he said them. We children didn't really understand what he was talking about, but we wanted to do what he was saying.

"Who is with me?" Dr. King asked, and all of us stood up, clapping. By the time we left that meeting, Dr. King had a commitment from me and everyone else in that church to do whatever it would take, nonviolently, to get the right to vote.

At that time I was already in the movement—the civil rights movement. I was mostly following the high school kids around—especially Bettie Fikes. She had this beautiful voice and I wanted to sing like her. Bettie and her friends were trying to integrate Selma by going to whites-only places. They sat at the whites-only Dairy Queen and the lunch counter at Woolworth's department store. They tried to sit downstairs at the movie theater. (Blacks could only sit in the balcony then.)

They said I couldn't take part in these sit-ins because I was too young, but I had a job to do. My job was to go for help. I was called the "gopher," because I always had to "go for" someone's mama when Bettie and her friends were put in jail.

That all changed on January 2, 1965. That's when Dr. King came back to Selma for a big mass meeting at Brown Chapel. We called it Emancipation Day because it was all about freedom. There were about seven hundred people there, and I was one of them. It was an awesome thing, a fearsome thing to see so many people. They had come from all around. And they had to travel some dangerous roads to get to Selma—little country roads where the Ku Klux Klan was riding around.

The music was fantastic. By then we had formed a freedom choir, and I was part of it. I got to sing in the choir with Bettie Fikes, and you know how I felt about that.

When Dr. King walked in, everyone stood and cheered. He talked about the vote and how we would get it. He told us we must be ready to march. His voice grew louder as he continued. "We must be ready to go to jail by the thousands." By the end he shouted, "Our cry . . . is a simple one. Give us the ballot!"

To tell you the truth, I just felt that once our parents got the right to vote, everything would be a whole lot better. There's power in a vote. For years black people tried to register to vote, but they were mostly turned away. Just for trying to register, they could lose their jobs. You see, whenever a black person tried to register, someone would take a picture and then show it to that person's boss. White people could fire black people whenever and however they wanted.

That's why the civil rights leaders needed us children to march. After Dr. King's speech, our local leaders planned two or three marches for us every day. They would say, "We're going to march to the courthouse tomorrow. If you're with us, come here to Brown Chapel at nine thirty."

The very first time I heard that, I said, "I'm going to march."

On the day of a march, you would go to school for attendance, then slip out and make it down to Brown Chapel. Our teachers were the ones who unlocked the back door and let us out of school. They supported us—they had our backs.

Our teachers were excellent, but these smart people could not vote. They couldn't pass the voter registration test. The tests were written to keep black people from voting. (White people didn't usually take those tests at all.) The registrars asked ridiculous questions such as, "How deep is the Alabama River?" and "How many jelly beans are in this gallon jar?" The questions had nothing to do with voting or the Constitution or citizenship.

Two or three times a day, a group of us students would leave Brown Chapel heading downtown. I don't think we were ever fewer than about fifty kids on a march. Before we left, the adults would tell us, "You're going to go to jail. Do not fight back. You might be pushed; you might be hit. Just turn the other cheek. Do not fight back. Don't worry about it. We'll take care of you."

Most of the time, once we got downtown the police let us march for four or five blocks. Then they would march us right onto yellow school buses. If you didn't get on the bus fast enough, the police would shock you with a cattle prod. That's a stick with an electrical charge, sort of like a Taser is now. Farmers used them to push cattle to move quicker or to get out of the way. That's what they used on us, like we were cattle.

At first they would take us to the old National Guard Armory, where we had to stand for hours all packed together, or sit on the concrete floor. But after a week or so of that, they started taking us right to jail.

CHAPTER 3
JAILBIRDS

The first time I went to jail I was fourteen, and I was scared. I didn't know what they were going to do with us. There must have been about a hundred boys and girls that time. All us girls were packed into one cell meant for two people. There were two iron beds coming out from the wall. And they didn't have mattresses on them, so they'd be really uncomfortable for the prisoners. Over in one corner was a sink. And there was a toilet, just a toilet bowl. There was no way to shield yourself from whoever was walking down past the cells, so we shielded each other.

After that first time, I wasn't so afraid, because I was with my buddies and we knew we had each other's back. What we could *do* with each other's backs, I don't know. Those white policemen had billy clubs and guns. But we held on to each other, and we figured there was safety in numbers.

Student protesters at the George Washington Carver Homes

It helped when we sang "We Shall Overcome." Singing those words made us believe we could do it. We could overcome the hate and racism. Every time I sang the line "We are not afraid," I lied a little, but it was important to sing it. The people who weren't afraid sang it the strongest and the loudest. The sound of their voices was like a warm blanket on a cold night. It made me feel a little stronger and more protected. Then I could sing a little louder too.

We sang it to let everyone know: We were on our way. We would not be ignored, and we would not be stopped.

Everything about the marches was well organized. The night before, the leaders would say, "We're going to have three demonstrations tomorrow. We'll need the first seventy-five kids here to go out by nine thirty. Second march, we're going to send ya'll out about twelve fifteen. Third march, ya'll are going to leave about three o'clock." We all knew ahead of time when there were going to be marches, so we could pick the march we wanted to go on.

We learned the drill real quick: We went to jail, we came back out, and then we went to jail again, be it that same day or the next day. Pretty soon we knew to take our own little bologna sandwiches and peanut butter and jelly sandwiches and cheese sandwiches and cookies and all the penny candy we could get, because jail food just wasn't good. If one of our parents or grandparents worked as someone's maid, they were bringing the white people's food home and giving it to us to take to jail with us. The white people never knew how much they had helped us.

My father didn't work in a white home.

He drove his own cab. He went and bought bologna so I would have those sandwiches to take to jail too. He was there for me; he wanted me to be safe. He told me, "If you see yourself in a situation where you will get hurt, come back home." He just told me to be careful. Be real careful.

With all the marching and going to jail, we kids were missing a lot of school. But we planned for that too. While we were marching, some kids stayed in school. They were the ones we called "the brains." And the brains actually did homework for the rest of us. They took tests for us too. (This was their way of taking part, even if they weren't marching.) Say I left to march, but there was a math test that day. Beatrice Torrey would stay at school and take my test, her test, and somebody else's test. Then during school lunch period, Beatrice would

leave for the next march. We had it all figured
out—and we were very determined.

Once, when the city jail was full, the police
took about three busloads of us kids to a
prison camp called Camp Selma. This prison
was about five miles away from town. After
about three days there they took us to another
prison camp even farther away. It was late at
night, and you couldn't see much. So at first we
thought they were taking us home,
back to Selma. But pretty soon
we knew we'd been riding too
long to be going back home.
I was scared, and I think
everybody on all three
buses was scared. We
were sure our parents
did not know where
we were. They didn't
know that we had

been put at a state prison camp! We were gone for six long days. Finally when our leaders in Selma found out where we were, they demanded our release. The buses brought us back to Selma, and we all ran home as fast as we could. We needed baths—and something to eat besides black-eyed peas!

That was the longest time I was ever in jail.

CHAPTER 4
IN THE SWEATBOX

For weeks we marched and we went to jail, over and over again. Then the police shot Jimmie Lee Jackson in a nearby town. I didn't know Jimmie Lee, but when I heard the news, I was scared for him and for us all. Jimmie Lee had been peacefully marching in Marion, thirty miles away. The marchers were singing freedom songs when the state troopers and police attacked them. As Jimmie Lee tried to protect his mother, a state trooper shot him in the stomach.

Marion was a real small town, so Jimmie Lee Jackson was brought to Selma. When we heard this, a lot of us headed for the Good Samaritan Hospital. (That was the hospital for black people then.) We all prayed Jimmie Lee Jackson would live.

While Jimmie Lee Jackson was in the hospital, it just seemed that everything got more dangerous. Even jail got more dangerous.

One day when a whole bunch of us went to jail, Pat Green got sick. We kept calling the jailers and asking for help, but all they did was bring us two brooms and tell us to clean up the place, saying it was filthy. There were twenty-three girls stuffed into this one cell.

Pat was moaning and groaning by this time, so I decided to try and get her some help. From the windows high up in the cell, you could look down and see people on Franklin Street.

I used one of the brooms to break the window. We shouted down that we had a sick girl who needed some help. That was all we were saying. We needed help for her.

Pretty soon the jailer and two deputies came in. "Okay," the jailer said, "who broke that window? You are in big trouble." (He actually called us by a bad name. White people called us that name a lot, to try and hurt us. But I don't say that word.)

Then he said we were all going to the sweat-box. None of us knew what he was talking about, but it didn't sound like a good place. He cursed and said, "I'm gonna ask you one more time, who broke that window."

So I answered, "I did."

"What's your name?"

I said "Lynda Blackmon."

Somebody behind me said, "*My* name's Lynda Blackmon." Somebody on the side said, "*My* name's Lynda Blackmon." Pretty soon there were about five Lynda Blackmons.

"All right, you all are trying to be smart— get up and move," he ordered.

He let Pat and one other girl stay in the cell. The rest of us were marched down a little hall-way to the sweatbox. The sweatbox didn't have any windows. It was an iron room with a big iron door.

They pushed us right in, closed the door, and locked it. I don't know how long we stayed in there. It could have been five minutes; it could have been five hours. All I know is every one of us passed out from the heat. There was no air. There was no bed. There was no toilet. There was no sink. There was nothing but heat in an iron box. It was dark too—there weren't any lights. We couldn't see anything. We didn't know anything.

When we came to, some other prisoners were carrying us out of the sweatbox into a courtroom. There was a judge there, and he said, "Y'all smell. Just write your name on a piece of paper and get out of here. If I see any one of you up here again, I'm gonna send you to juvenile detention." So I wrote a name from TV, like Howdy Doody. Others wrote names like Minnie Mouse, the Lone Ranger, or Tonto.

I doubt if anybody wrote her real name. All the judge wanted was to get us out of his courtroom.

By the time I got out of jail that day, Jimmie Lee Jackson had died.

I went straight to the funeral with my daddy. There were so many people there, we had to stand outside in the drizzling rain. It was hard to hear and I was too tired to listen. It was a long, sad, miserable day.

I learned that people were calling for a great

Funeral procession for Jimmie Lee Jackson

march. They wanted adults to march along with us kids in protest of Jackson's murder. It would be a whole new kind of march. A big march with everybody—adults along with us kids—on Sunday, March 7.

CHAPTER 5
BLOODY SUNDAY

When the day came, we set out from Brown Chapel as usual. I was with Jimmy Webb and fifteen of my buddies. Jimmy was our group leader. He told us to stick together and to remember "steady, loving confrontation."

When we got to the top of the Edmund Pettus Bridge going out of town, all I could see was a sea of white people. That's when I got nervous. The road was full of white men on foot and on horseback. They were state troopers and sheriffs' deputies. Along the road were white people sitting on their cars waving Confederate flags.

The deputies were just mean white men. They didn't have uniforms or anything. Our sheriff deputized any white man who might want to bust our heads. The harder you hit, the more popular you were with him. And Sheriff Clarke was the meanest of them all. He was a staunch segregationist. He believed that he was white and he was right, and that was it. He hated black men, women, and us black kids. He just hated us all.

At first I tried to tell myself it would be okay because there were so many of us. Then I saw the state troopers putting on gas masks and I got really scared. I'd only seen a gas mask on TV, but somehow I knew something dangerous was happening. I had never been in a violent situation before. Sure, we'd been hit with a billy club or cattle prod, but we'd never really been beaten. Suddenly this seemed like something very different.

"Go back to your church," the troopers bellowed out on bullhorns. "Go home."

Then Jimmy Webb said, "Let's pray," and we went down on our knees. That was normal.

You marched, you were stopped, you prayed. Then you turned around or went to jail.

So I was on my knees when I heard these sounds: *pop-pop, pop-pop*. All of a sudden a cloud of gas was burning my lungs and my eyes. I couldn't breathe and I couldn't see. It was terrifying. I didn't realize it then, but it was tear gas.

The next thing I knew, I felt a man's hand grab me from behind, pulling me backward. I heard him say that hateful word. Then I bit that hand and that's when he hit me over my eye. He hit me twice—hard. I was still kneeling, struggling to get up when he pushed me forward and hit me again, this time on the back of my head.

I staggered up and ran—right into the tear gas, but that big white man kept on running after me and hitting me. People were screaming and hollering and yelling. My heart was pounding so hard, I thought it would burst.

I must have fainted, because the next thing I knew, I came to on this stretcher. Some men were loading me into the back of a hearse, but I wasn't dead, and I sure wasn't going to let them put me in the back of that hearse before my time!

People were still running back across the bridge. The police and the state troopers were still beating them, and the air was thick with tear gas.

I jumped off the stretcher and started running toward home. I didn't know what I was doing; I just ran.

When I got across the bridge, that's when I saw my little sister Joanne. She'd been marching farther back. Now she looked like she was dead, lying in a man's arms.

I ran to him crying, "Oh she's dead. They killed my sister!" But he said she had just fainted, so I slapped her on the side of her face—you know, to wake her up. But when Joanne opened her eyes and looked at me, she started screaming. I knew tear gas had messed up my face, but I didn't realize I was covered in blood.

Troopers were everywhere and I was sure one was going to hit me again. So I grabbed Joanne's hand, jerked her up, and started running. We ran straight to Brown Chapel. But there was a wall in front of the church—a wall of troopers and policemen and people on horseback. They weren't letting anyone in or out. So I just kept running with Joanne. I wasn't ready to stop till we got to the First Baptist Church.

Lots of people were there who had been

hurt. We were told to wash our faces, necks, hands, and arms—any part that had been exposed to the tear gas. Everyone was trying to help us. When one man saw Joanne and me, he said, "This child is bleeding bad. She's got to go to the hospital." I didn't know who he was talking about, because Joanne wasn't bleeding. Then someone put a towel to my forehead and said, "She's bleeding from the back of her head too."

They took me to Good Samaritan Hospital, but there were white doctors there, and in my mind it was not a good day to be around white people. When the doctor sewed up my forehead, I felt every stitch. There were seven stitches over my eye and twenty-eight in the back of my head.

I didn't know it then, but while I was getting stitched up, people across the country were watching a special news report on TV. They saw what happened in Selma that day— the day reporters called Bloody Sunday.

When I woke up the next day, I was in a lot of pain, but mostly I was angry, really angry. I was angry with George Wallace. He was the governor of Alabama, and I felt like he had personally sent those state troopers to beat me up. The governor was supposed to be helping people in the state, protecting them, but he was hurting them. He was hurting *me*.

Then I heard that Dr. King was planning a march to Montgomery, the state capital, more than fifty miles away. Dr. King wanted to show Governor Wallace and the world that black people still demanded the right to vote—that beatings and violence would not stop us. But *I* wanted to go and show George Wallace what he had done to me. I wanted him to see my swollen face and my bandaged head. I wanted to let him know that he wasn't going to do that to me ever again.

When I told Daddy I wanted to go, he said no. It would be way too dangerous. But I pleaded and begged. He'd have to tie me up and lock me in the house to keep me from going, I told him.

Then Miz Marie Foster and Miz Mary Lamar and some other church ladies said they needed help on the trip. They promised Daddy they'd look after me. So finally, he said yes. It's a good thing he did, because I was going to go on that march no matter what! I was planning on running away and then taking whatever punishment my father gave me. Now I wouldn't have to worry that my daddy would be looking for me. He would know exactly where to find me.

While I was talking my daddy into letting me march, something amazing was happening in Selma. A whole lot of people who had seen that Bloody Sunday news report were so mad that they came to Selma to join us. We were inundated with people, all kinds of people. I mean housewives, teachers, students, priests, nuns . . . and many of them were white.

It was all so different from the segregation I was used to. It was a whole different feeling suddenly with white people living in your house. They marched with us and were willing to go to jail with us. They ate what we ate. We cooked collard greens and cornbread, and they ate it and enjoyed it as much as we did. They were happy to be with us, even if they had to sleep on the floor. I met a lady from Brooklyn named Edna Grabstein. Mrs. Viola Liuzzo from Detroit was staying at the house next door to us. A young lady from Canada named Lynn stayed at our house. It was amazing. These people were really concerned, and they wanted to help. There was a whole new feeling in Selma.

CHAPTER 6
HEADED FOR
MONTGOMERY

March 21 was Day One of the march and I was proud. We had finally won something. We won the right to march down the highway and be protected. The day was cloudy and misty, but the crowd at Brown Chapel was full of joy.

Dr. Martin Luther King and his wife, Coretta, were there and so were many others. Dr. King talked to the crowd about the importance of what we were about to do, but I wasn't listening. I just knew I was on my way to

At Brown Chapel, March 21, 1965

Montgomery to show George Wallace how he had hurt me. My stitches had been taken out, but the back of my head was still all shaved and bandaged and there was a smaller bandage over my eye. It was enough for him to see.

Daddy was there too. He told me to do the right thing and to mind folks. He told me he loved me and was proud of me.

People say we were three thousand strong

when we left the church singing "We Shall Overcome."

Just like the new feeling in Selma, there was a whole new feeling on this march. The white people didn't treat me any differently than they treated each other. It made me think that I wasn't really different. My grandmother had always told me that people were all the same. But when I walked outside the door in Selma each day, it was a different story.

Sometimes her lessons were hard to cling to, but that particular day was really mind blowing. I started looking at people a whole new way.

That first day of the march was really powerful. When we sang "Ain't Gonna Let Nobody Turn Me 'Round," it was true for the first time. At the bridge I saw soldiers protecting us with rifles. I was excited—and kind of amazed that I'd gotten that far without being beaten. Helicopters hovered above us. I felt even safer.

When we got to the top of the bridge, we

could see the road on the other side. This time, there were no state troopers blocking the way. The people who had been sitting along the sidelines on Bloody Sunday, waving their Confederate flags and calling out those ugly words, were not there either. Instead I saw army jeeps and men in green uniforms lining the highway. The press was there too, all around us. They were taking pictures and trying to ask us questions even though we were marching.

As we marched I felt relieved that I wasn't going to be hit again. I was beginning to realize what Bloody Sunday had done to my psyche. I still can't quite describe the fear I had felt that day.

After about five or six miles, most of the three thousand marchers had to go back to Selma. Only three hundred of us were permitted to march all the way to Montgomery. Of the

marchers going the whole distance, I was the youngest of them all. The other kids were around eighteen years old, but I was just one day short of my fifteenth birthday. I was ready too. In my backpack I had bologna and hot link sandwiches, cookies, plenty of candy, and some water. I also had clean underwear for three days.

After buses took the other marchers back to Selma, we walked about four more miles to our first campsite. It was on the farm that belonged to David and Rosa Bell Hall. There were big tents already set up—ladies in one tent and men in another. Our sleeping bags came in a truck that would drive with us during the whole march. (The truck had drinks and snacks for us to eat as we walked, and you could rest on the truck if you wanted to.) I remember we had spaghetti and meat sauce for dinner that night, all made for us by church ladies.

That first night it was hard to go to sleep in the big tent with all the women. The excitement about what we were doing and where we were going was still running very high. Everybody was just pumped up with this determination with a capital *D*. Of course, I was a little scared too. Sleeping on the ground like that, I thought a snake was going to bite me! And I was still kind of shocked that I had gone that far without being beaten again. I still had a fear of that, and pretty soon that fear was going to get me bad.

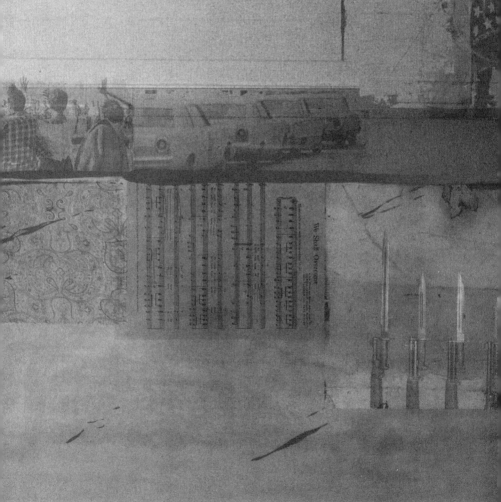

CHAPTER 7
TURNING 15

The next morning I woke up on the ground wrapped in a blanket, my head on the little canvas bag that held my stuff. All around me women were waking up, maybe 150 of them lying in long rows. It was March 22, 1965 — my fifteenth birthday.

When I left the tent, I walked out into a foggy, dreary morning. In front of me I saw three white National Guardsmen. Now, there were maybe a hundred guardsmen around, but I just focused on those three, because they were looking right at me, and the long steel bayonets on their rifles were pointed at me. In my eyes they looked exactly like the white troopers who had beaten me on Bloody Sunday. I started screaming and I couldn't stop. I was scared they were there to kill me, to finish the job they'd started two weeks before.

I was terrified. All I wanted to do was go home. I didn't care if George Wallace saw me or not. I didn't care if anybody ever voted, I just wanted to get back home to my daddy so he could protect me. Running back into the tent, I yelled, "They're going to kill me. Don't let them kill me! Please!" I grabbed Miz Mary, crying and yelling, "They're out there to kill me. I've got to go home."

People came running, and the National Guardsmen surrounded our tent. They wanted to know what was wrong too. Everyone wanted to know who was going to kill me. When I pointed to the guardsmen, people thought I was crazy. They're here to protect you, they said.

A lot of people wanted to send me home. They were mad because I was holding up the whole march. But the ladies said I was too scared to go anywhere. They tried to comfort me, to ease my fear. They talked about the significance of what we were doing and how far we had come in this struggle. But I could not be comforted. To me it was Bloody Sunday all over again. I was *that* scared.

Then a white man named Jim Letherer came over. He had lost a leg in a war and was walking all the way to Montgomery on two crutches. Jim told me that before he'd let anyone else harm another hair on my head, he would lie down and die for me. I knew I couldn't let this man do more for me than I could do for myself.

My grandmother used to say that if you

give in to something, if you give someone or something control over you, then you've given up yourself. And you couldn't do that. So I couldn't let George Wallace or my fear from having been beaten take control of me. If I did that, I would never become the person I wanted to be. And the person I wanted to be was a person who would stand up against what was wrong. I wanted not only to protect myself, but to protect others; not only to fight for myself, but to be out there fighting for others.

So at that moment I knew, if this man was willing to die for me, then I really had to give up the fear of dying myself. I knew I had to do this—and I *could* do it.

The march started one hour late that morning, but when it finally began, Jim Letherer and I marched and talked and sang freedom songs together down that highway.

I wasn't quite over my terror, though. I kept looking around. Every sudden movement or sound made me jump, and there was a lot going on. People in cars drove by yelling out racial slurs. Guardsmen were searching the woods and swamps for snipers. Dogs sniffed under every little bridge for bombs. Helicopters were always over us. There was a lot to be afraid of, but I just kept what my grandmother

Marchers John Lewis and Jim Letherer

told me in my mind. I knew I couldn't let fear of those white people take control of me.

As we marched that day we passed black people who lived along the way. They were on the sides of the road waving at us and yelling, "See you in Montgomery." And there was a little old wooden school where the children and the teachers were out there waving at us. They were just waving and singing "We Shall Overcome." That all felt nice, so we did have a good time.

Singing the freedom songs helped. "We Shall Overcome" was once just a dream for the future. But we were changing that and the songs helped us, they really did. Music is something that just stirs a person up. Back then the songs were emotional tools. They set our minds on what we were doing and why we were doing it. Everybody has a favorite song, and mine was "Woke Up This Morning with My Mind Stayed on Freedom." That was my song.

We sang "Ain't Gonna Let Nobody Turn Me 'Round" at different points of the day too. And always, always, no matter what, we sang "We Shall Overcome" to keep going.

As I walked that day, I knew each step was getting me closer to George Wallace. I was still afraid, but I wasn't terrified anymore. I was afraid when people talked about someone bombing the bridges and stuff. But I wasn't terrified for myself. Determination had entered into it instead. Determination is a way of over-coming terror. So by the end of the second day I felt fine. I was ready.

That evening we made it to our second campsite. People were tired—especially their feet. Most people had blisters, so we were all happy just to sit around. People talked, and we sang more songs. Some of the men played cards. It was just a nice time. Mostly the ground was wet, because it had drizzled rain all that day and the day before. But we went to sleep in those big tents again.

CHAPTER 8
WEARY
AND WET

Tuesday, Day Three, was the hard rain day. We were given these little orange ponchos to wear. Most of us had raincoats and umbrellas, but we wore the ponchos too.

That day we had to go through a dark swampy area. As we walked, the National Guardsmen scouted ahead, checking the woods and the swamp for snipers. Their dogs

searched for bombs. And helicopters stayed over us. You heard the helicopters every day and even at night during the march. They were looking for snipers too.

People came and joined the march during the day, and they'd go back home at night. At first most of the people were from Selma or the countryside nearby. But as we got closer to Montgomery, people from there came and joined the march.

Those people in cars still drove past us and yelled negative things—you know, the hateful stuff. But the National Guard kept the traffic flowing, so they couldn't stop. They had to keep going.

After two days of drizzling rain and then a whole day of hard rain, the ground was really soaked. Our campsite that night was so muddy, someone put down hay and then a plastic tarp over the hay. But I sank down into the mud anyway, and I wasn't the only one. We all woke up muddy. We joked that it was the heavy people who sank down in that mud, but I weighed about ninety pounds and I got just as muddy as the heavy people. It was a good thing a family nearby let me bathe in their house!

CHAPTER 9
MONTGOMERY AT LAST

On that fourth day of the march, thousands of people joined us as we got to the outskirts of Montgomery. There we stopped at the City of Saint Jude, a Catholic center where people began to gather.

It felt just awesome. I had done it. I had really done it. I was there. And then deep inside of me all the fear that something might happen to me—and the pain and anger that had driven me there—was released. I fell down on the ground and just cried and cried and cried.

I could not stop crying until I let it all out. And then it was gone. I was free.

Pretty soon even more people were pouring in from Selma, people who hadn't been allowed to make the whole march. It wasn't just us three hundred marchers anymore. They say by that night there were about ten thousand people in all. My sister Joanne came and lots of my friends. Daddy dropped them off and then went back to Selma to pick up more people. People were carpooling, because it was hard to get gas. The white service station wouldn't sell gas to blacks during the march. Daddy bought gas from the only black service station in Selma.

That night was amazing. All these famous singers and actors from Hollywood and New York City had come to Montgomery too: Harry Belafonte, Sammy Davis Jr., Pete Seeger, Tony Bennett, Nina Simone, Peter, Paul and Mary, and many more. There was this little stage set

John Lewis and other march leaders walking with Dr. King

At the Alabama State Capitol

up so they could perform for the crowd—for us. There had never been anything like that show in Alabama before.

The next morning, March 25, I knew I was going to see George Wallace and he was going to see me.

Everything was different that day. There were even more people now—more than twenty-five thousand. My buddies were there, kids I went to jail with so many times. And Daddy was there too. We were all singing and happy, marching to the capitol. We weren't walking two abreast anymore. Marchers filled the street. People had to squeeze in to join. There were so many of us, there wasn't room for people to stand on the sides and cheer us, but some people stood on the parked cars.

When I got to the capitol, I looked for Governor Wallace in the windows. They said he was behind the curtains peeping out, but I couldn't tell. I got as close as I could and shouted, "I'm here, Governor Wallace, I'm here!" So somebody in the governor's office surely got to see my bandages. Somebody did.

Dr. King at the capitol

There were lots of speakers, which made for a long, long day. Then it was over—what began on Bloody Sunday was done at last.

I went home to Selma and back to school. But I was a different person. We still had mass meetings, but we didn't march or go to jail anymore.

I learned a lot of things on that march, and one of them was about fear—how to respect it and how to embrace it. I also learned that I was not alone, that there were a lot of people— white as well as black—who really cared about what happened to me, Lynda Blackmon, and to the black people of Selma, Alabama.

I had learned so much, I just had to think about it all for a while. And while I was think- ing, something happened. On August 6, 1965, the United States Congress passed the Voting Rights Act. We had won! My buddies and I who had gone to jail so many times had won. Everyone on that march to Montgomery won.

We were determined to do something and we did it. If you are determined, you can overcome your fears, and then you can change the world.

The Selma Movement was a kids' movement. We didn't know it at the time, but we were making history. *You* have a voice too, and with determination, you can be a history maker just like me.

AIN'T GONNA LET NOBODY
TURN ME 'ROUND

Ain't gonna let nobody turn me 'round.

Turn me 'round, turn me 'round.

Ain't gonna let nobody turn me 'round.

I'm gonna keep on a-walkin', keep on

a-talkin'.

Marchin' on to freedom land.

Ain't gonna let no jailhouse turn me 'round.

Turn me 'round, turn me 'round.

Ain't gonna let no jailhouse turn me 'round.

I'm gonna keep on a-walkin'. keep on

a-talkin'.

Marchin' on to freedom land.

Ain't gonna let segregation turn me 'round.

Turn me 'round. turn me 'round.

Ain't gonna let segregation turn me 'round.

I'm gonna keep on a-walkin'. keep on

a-talkin'.

Marchin' on to freedom land.

WHY VOTING RIGHTS?

One hundred years before Bloody Sunday, the United States fought the Civil War over the rights of 3,950,528 Americans. The question was this: Were these enslaved men, women, and children people with rights guaranteed by the Constitution—or were they property? More than 600,000 soldiers, from North and South, died to decide that question.

The answer came when the United States Congress passed the Thirteenth Amendment, which ended slavery, and the Fourteenth and

Fifteenth Amendments, which guaranteed all the rights of citizenship. These rights had been denied us African Americans before: the right to marry, to own property, to be protected by law, to travel, to go to school, and to vote. Finally the Constitution said we had these rights and more.

But one hundred years later, there I was marching and going to jail for a right we had won so long ago, the right to vote. Why?

In places like Selma, state laws and procedures made registering to vote easy for white people, but close to impossible for African Americans. First you filled out a four-page application. Then you took an extremely difficult "literacy test," which white applicants usually did not have to take at all. And the registrars, who were all white, could decide that you'd failed even if you knew all the answers. Finally, you had to find a person who was already registered to "vouch" for you. After that you waited for days or weeks until the registrars decided—in their opinion—if you were fit to vote.

And that was not all. Just for trying to register, your photograph was taken and shown to your employer and your landlord. You could be fired from your job and evicted from your home. And then your picture was circulated to all the other employers and landlords so you could not get a new job or rent another home.

That's why my father could not vote. My grandmother could not vote. Even my teachers could not vote. In 1964 there were 14,400 white citizens and 15,115 black citizens eligible to vote in our county—more black than white citizens. But of the 9,530 people registered to vote, 9,195 were white. And that was after years of really brave people working to register African Americans.

So it was white voters who elected Governor George Wallace. His slogan was "Segregation now, segregation tomorrow, segregation forever!" White citizens elected our mayor Joe Smitherman, another segregationist. And they elected Sheriff Jim Clark—one of the meanest segregationists around.

All of this is why, time after time, Reverend Martin Luther King Jr. called out "Give us the ballot!" As he put it, "So long as I do not . . . possess the right to vote, I do not possess myself. I cannot make up my mind—it is made up for me. I cannot live as a democratic citizen, observing the laws I have helped to enact—I can only submit to the edict of others." He called our all-white government "democracy turned upside down."

This is why I went to jail and marched for the right to vote. This is why I rejoiced when the Voting Rights Act was passed in 1965. And why, the day I turned twenty-one (the voting age back then), I registered to vote.

It was a great feeling, registering, but for me to have that feeling, many people had paid a high price.

The voting rights movement started in Selma before I was even born. There was a group of people so brave, they were called the Courageous Eight. One of them, Amelia Boynton, had this big sign in her office that said A VOTELESS PEOPLE IS A HOPELESS PEOPLE. And I believe that, I really do.

It took tremendous determination to win the right to vote. You know how I was beaten and terrified. Many others were too. But three people lost their lives in the days before and after Bloody Sunday. They were murdered—and one friend disappeared. These are their stories:

Remember **JIMMIE LEE JACKSON**— the man who died while we were in jail? He was the youngest deacon of his church, an army veteran, and determined to vote. He tried to register over and over again—for four years.

On the night of February 18, he marched for that right, and for freedom of speech. (One of the movement's leaders was in jail for speaking out.) With Jackson were his mother, his eighty-two-year-old grandfather, and some four hundred others—all unarmed. The marchers were nervous because it was nighttime and there were more police than usual. Both police and state troopers were there. Even Sheriff Jim Clark from Selma was there. They had guns, clubs, and those electric cattle prods ready.

When the streetlights went out, they attacked, beating the men, women, youth, elders, even the press.

Many people tried to run to the church for shelter, but they were blocked by more police. So they rushed into local homes or businesses — anywhere they could get away. Jimmie Lee Jackson ran into a little café. There he tried to shield his grandfather (who was badly beaten) and his mother from the police. But a trooper shot Jimmie Lee Jackson in the stomach. He tried to run, but the troopers followed and continued to beat him until he fell to the ground. He died eight days later. Jimmie Lee Jackson was twenty-six years old and the father of a young daughter.

REVEREND REEB was a Unitarian minister from Boston, a white man, who came to Selma the Monday night after Bloody Sunday. He was one of many who answered

Martin Luther King's call for religious leaders to come and march for freedom the next day. On Tuesday some three thousand marchers followed King to the Edmund Pettus Bridge, where I had been beaten just two days before. They knelt in front of the troopers

who blocked their way, they prayed, and then they turned around. Afterward Reverend Reeb and two others went to a small black-owned café for dinner.

When the three ministers left the café, a group of white men attacked and beat them with baseball bats and clubs. Two days later, Reverend Reeb died from his injuries. He was thirty-eight years old and the father of four young children.

VIOLA LIUZZO was a white homemaker who drove all the way from Detroit because she was so upset about what was happening in Selma. I got to know her because she stayed with a family right near us in the GWC Houses.

After the big march, Mrs. Liuzzo drove back and forth between Montgomery and Selma to bring tired, happy marchers home. With her was someone I knew well, my neighbor Leroy Moten.

On one of the trips back to Montgomery, Mrs. Liuzzo's car was forced off the road by a carload of men—KKK members. The men shot her in the head, killing her instantly. Viola Liuzzo was thirty-nine years old and the mother of five children.

When the Klansmen shot Viola Liuzzo, they thought they'd killed **LEROY MOTEN** as well. But he had lain down underneath her bleeding body and stayed so still that the murderers thought he was dead too. That's the only reason Leroy wasn't murdered.

As soon as they could, people got Leroy out of Selma. They had to get him away from the Klansmen, who would have killed him for sure, because he was the only eyewitness to murder.

Leroy Moten was nineteen years old when he fled for his life, leaving his home, family, and friends behind. To this day, he lives safely far away from Selma.

On August 6, 1965, Congress passed the Voting Rights Act, enforcing the voting rights that had been guaranteed in the Fourteenth and Fifteenth Amendments. The new law said that in parts of the country where the right to vote was withheld, the federal government would review state or local laws and prevent any that discriminated against voters.

Since it was passed, the Voting Rights Act has been changed several times. In 2013 the Supreme Court struck down the part of the act that targeted places like Selma, where the right to vote was denied in the past. A majority of the justices said that discrimination was no longer a problem, so federal review was not needed. The justices who disagreed said the federal review prevented discrimination and that, without it, voting rights would become a problem again.

Who has the right to vote is still being decided today.

ACKNOWLEDGMENTS

I wish to thank my extraordinary grandmother, who gave me determination and courage; my husband, who stood by me and believed in me throughout this entire project; my children and grandchildren, whom I dearly love.—L.B.L.

As this book has three authors, we owe the greatest debt to each other. Our eternal thanks to Lynda for sharing her story, her life, and her friendship with us over these many years—and to one another for three decades of friendship and collaboration.—E.L. & S.B.

Our incalculable thanks to our stellar editor, Lauri Hornik, a kindred spirit from the beginning; designer Mina Chung for taking our dream and making it more beautiful than we imagined; wonderful artist PJ Loughran for revealing what was never photographed and making us cry; and the entire team at Dial Books for Young Readers for all of their support for our book.

We would not be holding this book in our hands without our extraordinary agent, Charlotte Sheedy, who believed in this book from the beginning (and our gratitude to our great friend Karen Shatzkin, for introducing us to Charlotte in the first place); Mackenzie Brady, who was always on top of everything in spite of us all; and our families and friends who have kept the faith.

The authors also wish to honor and acknowledge:
• Dr. Amelia Boynton-Robinson and the other members of the Courageous Eight: Mr. Ulysses Blackmon, Mr. Earnest L. Doyle, Mrs. Marie Foster, Mr. James Edward Gildersleeve, Rev. J. D. Hunter, Dr. F. D. Reese, and Rev. Henry

Shannon Jr., who bravely fought for voting rights in Selma before the time covered in this story

• Reverend Dr. Martin Luther King Jr., Fred Shuttlesworth, and other members of the Southern Christian Leadership Conference (SCLC) who came to Selma to inspire and help organize the voting rights movement

• John Lewis, Bernard and Colia LaFayette and other young members of the Student Nonviolent Coordinating Committee (SNCC) who risked their lives to lead the youth and young adults in the movement. It was John Lewis and Hosea Williams (SCLC) who led the march across the Edmund Pettus Bridge toward the waiting troopers and possemen on Bloody Sunday.

• The many Hollywood and Broadway performers and activists, especially Harry Belafonte and Bayard Rustin, who helped make the March to Montgomery such an extraordinary event.

• And all the youth and young adults who so bravely faced violence and jail.

PHOTO CREDITS

14, 45, 48, 72, 114: © Bettmann/CORBIS

22, 34: © John Kouns/syndicjournal.us

55, 99: © 1965 Spider Martin

56, 57, 70, 92, 116, 118: © Associated Press

83, 84: © Matt Herron/The Image Works

74, 86, 100: © Bruce Davidson/Magnum Photos

91, 101: © AL.com/Landov

98: Peter Pettus, Library of Congress

113: Photographer unknown, every effort has been made to locate copyright holders

DISCUSSION GUIDE

TO OUR READERS

LIVING WITH SEGREGATION

LEARNING ABOUT NONVIOLENCE

HOW KIDS MADE HISTORY

THE VOTING RIGHTS MOVEMENT

RACISM THEN AND RACISM NOW

TO OUR READERS

FROM LYNDA

My wish is for you the reader to know that you can make a difference. You were born courageous. Don't let anyone take that from you. I want you to understand that with Steady Loving Confrontation, you can work to change whatever you see that is wrong. Those words from Dr. Martin Luther King, Jr. are three powerful words that can carry you far. They have carried me for over fifty years. They carried a movement for voting rights to victory. They carried a movement for civil rights to victory, not only in the United States of America, but internationally.

Think *steady*—change doesn't happen overnight. Don't stop if you see no result the next week or month. Strive on. Let no person or thing turn you around. When you believe in yourself, you will achieve your wildest dreams. Think *loving*— let others feel positive about what you care about, and they will join you. You can be powerful, make change, and be consistent with your nonviolent fight. I know so many of you may be saying it's hard to be nonviolent, with all the violence, racism, prejudices, and hatred going on in this country and around the world today. How can we turn the other cheek? Why should we? The answer to those questions comes from my grandmother, Sylvia Johnson. She used to say, don't act a fool because someone else does. Violence on violence gets you killed. But Steady Loving Confrontation for me and thousands of others got results. It was fantastic knowing that I took part in giving the right to vote to so many even though I wasn't old enough to vote myself.

I want you to take away from my story the knowledge that many people were beaten and some died in the struggle to gain the right to vote. So not voting is unacceptable! Make sure that the people in your home or community who are eligible to vote are registered. And come election time, don't let anything stop them from voting.

I want you to take away that you can be powerful at any age. At seven years of age I vowed that somehow, by the time I got big, no one would grow up without a mommy because of the color of her skin. At fourteen, I was on the Edmund Pettus Bridge making history. And at twenty-one, I voted.

I want you to take away the belief that change can still happen today, because it has happened before. I want you to know what growing up with segregation was really like so you can see how much has changed and not get discouraged. Segregation had an impact on how you shopped, where you ate, the schools you went to, even how you walked down the street. And back then groups like the KKK got away with hate crimes. So a lot has changed.

For the writers among you, I would like to say mine is not the only story—there are so many more great stories from this turning point in history. There are stories about people from SNCC like Colia, Bernard Lafayette's wife. She is a beautiful lady. James Bevel from SCLC, James Orange, James Webb, Hosea Williams. There are stories about the older kids like Cleophus Hobbs, Charles Bonner, Terry Shaw, Bettie Mae Fikes, Bennie Ruth Crenshaw, Hazel Chapman, and Charles Mauldin, who were the ones sitting in at lunch counters, ice cream shops, and downstairs at the movies. These stories still need to be written, by someone just like you.

And lastly—for those of you who have suffered trauma like me, a special message. When violence did happen on March 7th I found that I was not mentally prepared for the severity of the beating or of the nightmares that followed for years and years afterward. It took talking about it over and over until I could share the whole story. But once I started sharing my story, the healing began, and then I was even more able to help others.

FROM ELSPETH AND SUSAN

When we first met Lynda—on the phone—we knew that hers was a story we wanted to share. Not only did we love her from the first, but she had all of the "ingredients" for the Selma story: She had struggled with racism. She was inspired by the words of Dr. King when she was just thirteen. She marched and went to jail for voting rights as a young teenager. She was badly beaten on Bloody Sunday. And she was the youngest person of the three hundred allowed to make the full march from Selma to Montgomery. But more important than all of that is how Lynda processed her experiences into a message of determination and hope, a commitment to nonviolence and to the ability of "steady, loving confrontation" to create change. We are proud to have helped Lynda bring her remarkable story to readers like you.

LIVING WITH SEGREGATION

Q: LYNDA, HOW DID SEGREGATION AFFECT YOUR LIFE GROWING UP?

Segregation was a hard pill to swallow. It felt like segregation was designed to make you feel less than human. You were told that in the names you were called, like the "n word." Or at the water fountains, where there was a sign that said COLORED ONLY and another sign that said WHITES ONLY. The colored water fountain would usually be a water fountain about the size of a child's water fountain and the white water fountain would be tall. When you went to the movies, black people had to sit in the balcony. You couldn't sit at lunch counters either. And at the ice cream store you had to go to a window at the back to get your ice cream.

Going shopping in Selma during segregation was something else. If you were black, you were not allowed to try on a clothing item, be it a dress, skirt, blouse, shoes, whatever. When you walked in the store, people used to call you the "n word" and ask what you wanted. They wouldn't let us try on anything because then white people wouldn't want to wear it! Say you wanted a new pair of shoes. The salesperson would look at your foot and guess the size.

Not everything about segregation was bad. Our schools were segregated but I loved school. Our schoolbooks were passed down to us after years of use in the white schools. Some had pages missing, but we still managed to learn, because we had strong, smart, caring black teachers who made sure of it. So did the strong families and others who made sure we went to school. Growing up in the George Washington Carver Homes was like growing up in a village. Everyone seemed to feel responsible for everyone else. We always felt safe and protected.

Still, when people ask me about how segregation affected me, I just let them know that my mother died because of the color of her skin. If she had been allowed to go to the white hospital, her life could have been saved. Segregation destroyed my family and it hurt a lot of people.

THINK ABOUT IT

1. In 1896 the Supreme Court ruled that facilities could be segregated or separated by race as long as they were equal. Laws did not overturn this "separate but equal" policy until 1954. Think about the situations Lynda describes from her childhood. How was separate *not* equal?

2. Lynda's grandmother taught her that there was no one in the world any better than she was. How would remembering this help you deal with segregation?

3. In *Turning 15* Lynda talks about the sense of community in her childhood. How would that help you deal with discrimination today?

4. How did you feel when you read Lynda's descriptions of segregation? Have you ever been made to feel "less than" others? What was your reaction?

LEARNING ABOUT NONVIOLENCE

Q: LYNDA, HOW AND WHEN DID YOU LEARN ABOUT NONVIOLENCE?

Well, I first heard about nonviolence in early 1963 when I was just thirteen years old. Mr. Bernard Lafayette had come to Selma with the Student Nonviolent Coordinating Committee (SNCC). He was teaching the high school kids like Bettie Fikes about nonviolence, and I tagged along. That was the first time I heard that word, "nonviolence." He talked about being confronted and standing still and being in control of your emotions, not letting someone see the hurt or the anger or whatever emotion that person was trying to cause in you. Once when he first came to Selma, Bernard Lafayette was beaten up by some white men. Every time they knocked him down, he stood up again, until finally they stopped. He wore his bloody shirt around town for the next couple of days, just so people could see what had been done to him.

Then I heard Dr. King when he came to Selma in 1963. (That was before the big meeting in January 1965.) Dr. King talked about nonviolence too, but he said it a little differently. He kept talking about steady, loving confrontation. He talked about how the Bible says to turn the other cheek if someone hits you, but Dr. King said you shouldn't only turn the other cheek, you should turn the other side of your body. And you had to listen with your heart and not just your ears.

By the time the marches started, we were a disciplined group of children. When the leaders took us younger kids for training, they would stand close to us and yell the "n word" while pushing us off our seats. They pretended to kick us as we fell to the floor and put their faces so close to ours it would seem like they were actually spitting on us. They would pour a glass of water on us, and we had to pretend it was hot coffee even though it really wasn't. By January 1965, we knew how to drop to our knees, roll into a fetal position, and tuck our heads to our knees and cover them with our arms.

Bernard Lafayette and Dr. King had taught us as children that violence was not only being hit physically but it was mental abuse as well. What they taught me about nonviolence was in my head and my heart on Bloody Sunday. I did not think about returning the pain of being beaten because I was so tuned in to turning the other cheek. (Well, I did bite the hand of the man who was beating me . . .but that was all!)

THINK ABOUT IT

1. How did the philosophy of nonviolence guide the voting rights movement in Selma?

2. In *Turning 15* Lynda talks about the importance of Dr. King's words: "steady, loving confrontation." How did Lynda translate this idea into action? How can you imagine using this idea?

3. What challenges would you find in following a philosophy of nonviolence?

HOW KIDS MADE HISTORY

Q: LYNDA, HOW IS IT THAT YOU WERE MARCHING AND GOING TO JAIL AT SUCH A YOUNG AGE?

The voting rights movement in Selma was a kids' movement because it had to be. Adults couldn't fill the jails. They had families to care for and jobs to hold on to. The movement leaders knew they had to send us kids to march, face the police, and fill the jails.

Q: WHAT MADE SO MANY KIDS STRONG ENOUGH TO FACE THE RACE HATRED AND KEEP GOING?

We knew the movement leaders had our backs from Martin Luther King, Jr. to the young men and women from SNCC. But I would say the entire black community had our backs: the teachers who unlocked the school doors for us, the assistant principal Reverend Frederick Reese, and our parents who packed food for us to take to jail. But most importantly, we had each other's backs. I remember a few bullies in elementary school. But when we started to march they were with us. They were in the same boat as the rest of us and none of us could swim, so we had to hold each other up to keep from going down. It was all for one and one for all. That made us stronger and braver. There was safety in numbers too. I don't think I ever went to jail with fewer than fifty kids. And singing together always made us braver than we really were. Songs such as "We Shall Overcome" definitely helped us stay determined.

Q: WHEN DID YOU REALIZE THAT YOU MADE HISTORY?

I don't think any of us knew we were making history at the time. I know that I didn't. I was just determined to right a wrong that had been done to me and my family when my mother died, and I had a vow in my mind that no one would lose a loving parent like that again.

It was not until maybe twenty-five years later when the National Voting Rights Museum and Institute opened in Selma and I was telling my story of Bloody Sunday into a microphone that I began to realize that we—all of us who marched and went to jail—had made history, the kind that's written in books and shown in movies.

Q: THE KIDS IN SELMA WERE VERY WELL ORGANIZED. WHO WAS RESPONSIBLE FOR THAT?

Members of SNCC trained us to organize ourselves. First they trained the young adults. Some of these people, such as Bettie Mae Fikes had already graduated from high school. These were the people we respected and looked up to. They got the younger kids involved, and once they were trained they brought in new kids.

THINK ABOUT IT

1. You see an injustice, you join a group, or organize one yourself. Describe what you think are the most important characteristics for the group to have in order to be successful.

2. How are the characteristics of a successful group today the same or different from the Selma movement of 1965?

THE VOTING RIGHTS MOVEMENT

Q: WHO STARTED THE VOTING RIGHTS MOVEMENT IN SELMA?

It really all began with the Courageous Eight. Reverend Frederick Reese and Ms. Amelia Boynton and six others were part of the Courageous Eight. They were like the self-appointed leaders in the black community. They were the people who were fighting hard for things. They also were educated people. It was the Courageous Eight who invited Dr. King to come to Selma.

People like my father and grandmother went to classes run by the Courageous Eight, classes to help you pass the test to register to vote. It was like a civics class. They had classes two or three times a week.

Q: WHEN DID CIVIL RIGHTS LEADERS COME TO SELMA?

I was thirteen when Bernard Lafayette came to town. He was one of the founders and leaders of the Student Nonviolent Coordinating Committee (SNCC)—we called it "snick." He formed a SNCC chapter in Selma with some of the older kids, and in 1963–64 they started sitting in at lunch counters and movie theaters. Bernard Lafayette was teaching nonviolence. I tagged along and learned too.

After the events in Birmingham in 1963, I think Dr. King and others looked at the different problems African Americans were facing, and they connected voting rights to civil rights. It was like what the sign in Ms. Boynton's office said: A VOTE-LESS PEOPLE IS A HOPELESS PEOPLE. Dr. King, SCLC (the

Southern Christian Leadership Conference, Dr. King's group), and SNCC were like movie directors. They came in 1963 and 1964 and started directing this "movie" and it was finished on March 21, 1965, when we actually left Selma marching to Montgomery.

Dr. King was also like a general, and Hosea Williams and Ralph Abernathy and others were his lieutenants. Every good general has to have some good officers. Dr. King left them in Selma that winter of 1965. They stayed to keep spirits high and keep us working.

THINK ABOUT IT

1. Find out more about the events in Birmingham, Alabama, in 1963. What were people protesting in Birmingham? What role did young people play in those protests? Compare the issues and events in Birmingham and Selma.

2. Lynda describes the events of the Selma Voting Rights Movement as a movie. Imagine that you are making a movie about the Selma movement. What scenes would you show? Pick one to describe in detail. Describe the characters, the setting, and the actions.

3. Lynda talks about Dr. King as the general. Are there leaders you admire today? Describe them and explain why you admire them.

RACISM THEN AND RACISM NOW

Q: LYNDA, WHAT DID YOU THINK OF RACISM AND WHITE PEOPLE BEFORE THE MOVEMENT?

My mother died because she was black. It was a white racist who tried to kill me on the Edmund Pettus Bridge. In the South you're born knowing there is no love for you from the other race. You learned to avoid white people as much as possible, to get out of their line of fire. When a white person walked toward you, you stepped off the sidewalk—like you had a disease or something.

My daddy was a big strong black man who walked tall and proud, shoulders back, hat on. But I remember when he and I entered a store and some little white girl called him that "n word." His hat came off and his whole body slumped down. White people showed us no respect at all. We heard of terrorist groups like KKK burning crosses and beating, sometimes killing people. No one would say anything when white people did that. It was a fact of life to some people, especially those who lived in rural areas. I do believe growing up I was learning to hate white people.

Q: HOW DID YOUR VIEWS CHANGE AFTER BLOODY SUNDAY?

There had been white outsiders in Selma before Bloody Sunday and they seemed friendly and concerned. But to me they had to have some ulterior motive so I stayed away from them.

But after Bloody Sunday, that's when you really saw a lot of white people. They were the same color as those white people who treated me badly, but these white people were sitting in my house, and eating with me and laughing and crying with me and going to jail and marching. It was just a whole other experience that showed me a new way to look at life. These people came here to fight for all people. It was no longer just me, a black person fighting for other black people. It was all for one and one for all. So it changed me. It changed my heart. I became the person fighting for people. Period.

Q: WHAT WOULD YOU LIKE TO SHARE WITH YOUNG PEOPLE TODAY?

The color thing is still very much alive and running rampant all over this United States. It is causing one sad tragedy after another, which is why I appreciate the Black Lives Matter movement. I would like to say to young people that it is time for change again. And as I said, whatever wrongs you see you can change with steady, loving confrontation. Don't stop when you get tired or discouraged, stay determined, that's the steady part. Don't give in to the hate—stay positive. That's the loving part. And stand up to the bullying with the power of your people. That is confrontation.

THINK ABOUT IT

1. Understanding the racial experiences of a group is difficult—even if it is your own group. For example, a person who grows up with white privilege is usually not aware of their privilege because it appears normal to them. Lynda

gained a new understanding of race after Bloody Sunday. Describe a situation that could or did give you insight into the experience of another ethnic group or race.

2. Think of something that needs changing. Describe how the practice of steady, loving confrontation could be applied to make the change.